Clean Cuss Words Adult Coloring Book
28 Fun Images to Freshen Up Your Potty Mouth
28 Fun Images of Clean Cuss Words

FUDGE
NUGGETS!

KEY
DARN

Oh Bug
Butts

Shitake Mushrooms

Sugar.
Honey.
Iced.
Tea.

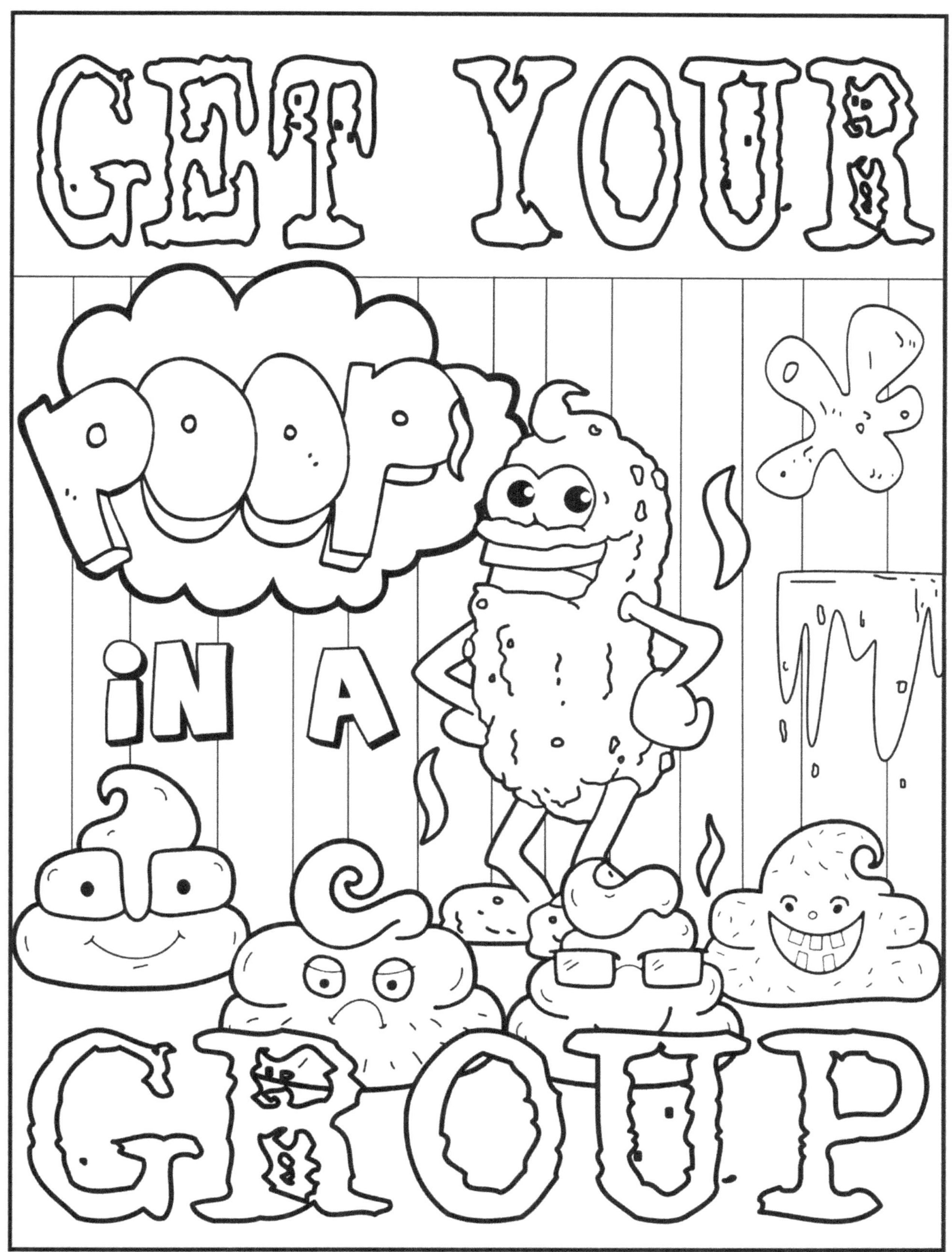

GET YOUR
POOP
IN A
GROUP

Holy Guacamole

OH
FUDGE
BAR

SHUT YOUR
PIE HOLE

CRUD,
MUFFIN

Go Lick
A Duck

Jack Donkey

Pickle
Head

Snub
of
an
iTCH!

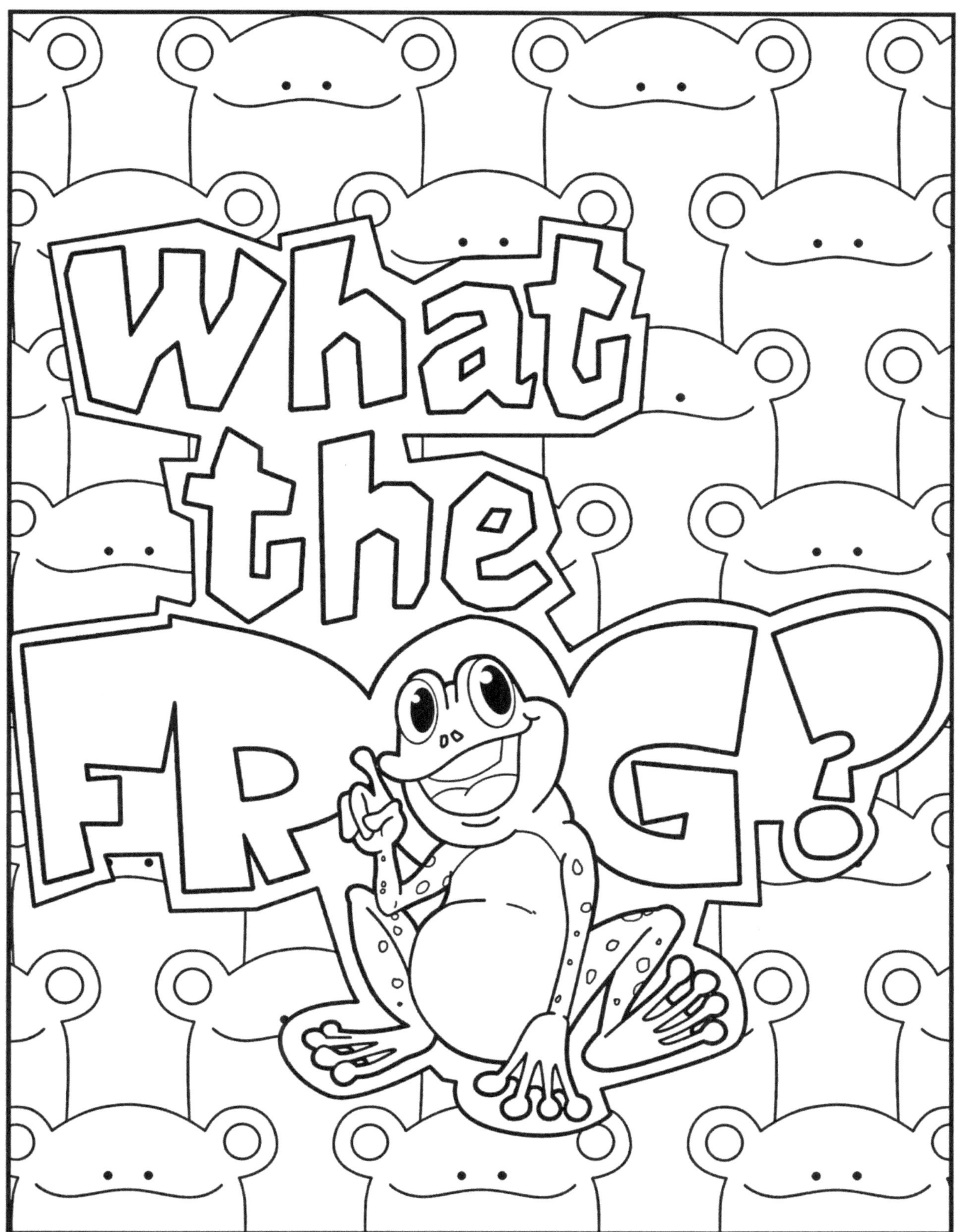

What the
FROG?

FISH
PASTE

MOTHER
TRUC
KER

Raspberries!

SON OF A
MOTHERLESS
GOAT

FRAZZLE
RAZZLE

hasenpfeffer

NUCKIN
FUTS

RATS!

Stink
ON A
Stick

SUNNY
BEACH

Bullspit!

www.ingramcontent.com/pod-product-compliance
Lightning Source LLC
Chambersburg PA
CBHW081600270726
48657CB00029B/3435